THE ELDEST

A DOMESTIC DRAMA IN THREE ACTS

BY

JOHN GALSWORTHY

NEW YORK
CHARLES SCRIBNER'S SONS
1916

AUTHOR'S NOTE

The Eldest Son was written in the early months of 1909. Accidents happy and unhappy have prevented its performance earlier than November of 1912.

ACT I

SCENE I

The scene is a well-lighted, and large, oak-panelled hall, with an air of being lived in, and a broad, oak staircase. The dining-room, drawing-room, billiard-room, all open into it: and under the staircase a door leads to the servants' quarters. In a huge fireplace a log fire is burning. There are tiger-skins on the floor, horns on the walls; and a writing-table against the wall opposite the fireplace. FREDA STUDDENHAM, *a pretty, pale girl with dark eyes, in the black dress of a lady's-maid, is standing at the foot of the staircase with a bunch of white roses in one hand, and a bunch of yellow roses in the other. A door closes above, and* SIR WILLIAM CHESHIRE, *in evening dress, comes downstairs. He is perhaps fifty-eight, of strong build, rather bull-necked, with grey eyes, and a well-coloured face, whose choleric autocracy is veiled by a thin urbanity. He speaks before he reaches the bottom.*

SIR WILLIAM. Well, Freda! Nice roses. Who are they for?

FREDA. My lady told me to give the yellow to Mrs. Keith, Sir William, and the white to Miss Lanfarne, for their first evening.

3

SIR WILLIAM. Capital. [*Passing on towards the drawing-room*] Your father coming up to-night?

FREDA. Yes.

SIR WILLIAM. Be good enough to tell him I specially want to see him here after dinner, will you?

FREDA. Yes, Sir William.

SIR WILLIAM. By the way, just ask him to bring the game-book in, if he's got it.

> *He goes out into the drawing-room; and* FREDA *stands restlessly tapping her foot against the bottom stair. With a flutter of skirts* CHRISTINE KEITH *comes rapidly down. She is a nice-looking, fresh-coloured young woman in a low-necked dress.*

CHRISTINE. Hullo, Freda! How are *you?*

FREDA. Quite well, thank you, Miss Christine—Mrs. Keith, I mean. My lady told me to give you these.

CHRISTINE. [*Taking the roses*] Oh! Thanks! How sweet of mother!

FREDA. [*In a quick, toneless voice*] The others are for Miss Lanfarne. My lady thought white would suit her better.

CHRISTINE. They suit *you* in that black dress.

[FREDA *lowers the roses quickly.*

What do you think of Joan's engagement?

FREDA. It's very nice for her.

CHRISTINE. I say, Freda, have they been going hard at rehearsals?

FREDA. Every day. Miss Dot gets very cross, stage-managing.

CHRISTINE. I do hate learning a part. Thanks awfully for unpacking. Any news?

FREDA. [*In the same quick, dull voice*] The under-keeper, Dunning, won't marry Rose Taylor, after all.

CHRISTINE. What a shame! But I say that's serious. I thought there was—she was—I mean——

FREDA. He's taken up with another girl, they say.

CHRISTINE. Too bad! [*Pinning the roses*] D'you know if Mr. Bill's come?

FREDA. [*With a swift upward look*] Yes, by the six-forty.

> RONALD KEITH *comes slowly down, a weathered firm-lipped man, in evening dress, with eyelids half drawn over his keen eyes, and the air of a horseman.*

KEITH. Hallo! Roses in December. I say, Freda, your father missed a wigging this morning when they drew blank at Warnham's spinney. Where's that litter of little foxes?

FREDA. [*Smiling faintly*] I expect father knows, Captain Keith.

KEITH. You bet he does. Emigration? Or thin air? What?

CHRISTINE. Studdenham'd never shoot a fox, Ronny. He's been here since the flood.

KEITH. There's more ways of killing a cat—eh, Freda?

CHRISTINE. [*Moving with her husband towards the drawing-room*] Young Dunning won't marry that girl, Ronny.

KEITH. Phew! Wouldn't be in his shoes, then! Sir William'll never keep a servant who's made a scandal in the village, old girl. Bill come?

> *As they disappear from the hall,* JOHN LATTER *in a clergyman's evening dress, comes sedately downstairs, a tall, rather pale young man, with something in him, as it were, both of heaven, and a drawing-room. He passes* FREDA *with a formal little nod.* HAROLD, *a fresh-cheeked, cheery-looking youth, comes down, three steps at a time.*

HAROLD. Hallo, Freda! Patience on the monument. Let's have a sniff! For Miss Lanfarne? Bill come down yet?

FREDA. No, Mr. Harold.

> HAROLD *crosses the hall, whistling, and follows* LATTER *into the drawing-room. There is the sound of a scuffle above, and a voice crying: "Shut up, Dot!" And* JOAN *comes down screwing her head back. She is pretty and small, with large clinging eyes.*

JOAN. Am I all right behind, Freda? That beast, Dot!

FREDA. Quite, Miss Joan.

> DOT'S *face, like a full moon, appears over the upper banisters. She too comes running down, a frank figure, with the face of a rebel.*

DOT. You little *being!*

JOAN. [*Flying towards the drawing-room, is overtaken at the door*] Oh! Dot! You're pinching!

> *As they disappear into the drawing-room, MA-BEL LANFARNE, a tall girl with a rather charming Irish face, comes slowly down. And at sight of her FREDA's whole figure becomes set and meaning-full.*

FREDA. For you, Miss Lanfarne, from my lady.

MABEL. [*In whose speech is a touch of wilful Irishry*] How sweet! [*Fastening the roses*] And how are *you*, Freda?

FREDA. Very well, thank you.

MABEL. And your father? Hope he's going to let me come out with the guns again.

FREDA. [*Stolidly*] He'll be delighted, I'm sure.

MABEL. Ye-es! I haven't forgotten his face—last time.

FREDA. You stood with Mr. Bill. He's better to stand with than Mr. Harold, or Captain Keith?

MABEL. He didn't touch a feather, that day.

FREDA. People don't when they're anxious to do their best.

> *A gong sounds. And MABEL LANFARNE, giving FREDA a rather inquisitive stare, moves on to the drawing-room. Left alone without the roses, FREDA still lingers. At the slamming of a door above, and hasty footsteps, she shrinks back against the stairs. BILL runs down, and comes on her suddenly. He is a tall, good-looking*

*edition of his father, with the same stubborn
look of veiled choler.*

BILL. Freda! [*And as she shrinks still further back*]
What's the matter? [*Then at some sound he looks round
uneasily and draws away from her*] Aren't you glad to
see me?

FREDA. I've something to say to you, Mr. Bill.
After dinner.

BILL. Mister——?

*She passes him, and rushes away upstairs. And
BILL, who stands frowning and looking after
her, recovers himself sharply as the drawing-
room door is opened, and SIR WILLIAM and
MISS LANFARNE come forth, followed by
KEITH, DOT, HAROLD, CHRISTINE, LATTER,
and JOAN, all leaning across each other, and
talking. By herself, behind them, comes LADY
CHESHIRE, a refined-looking woman of fifty,
with silvery dark hair, and an expression at
once gentle, and ironic. They move across the
hall towards the dining-room.*

SIR WILLIAM. Ah! Bill.

MABEL. How do you do?

KEITH. How are you, old chap?

DOT. [*gloomily*] Do you know your part?

HAROLD. Hallo, old man!

*CHRISTINE gives her brother a flying kiss. JOAN
and LATTER pause and look at him shyly without speech.*

BILL. [*Putting his hand on* JOAN'S *shoulder*] Good luck, you two! Well mother?

LADY CHESHIRE. Well, my dear boy! Nice to see you at last. What a long time!

> *She draws his arm through hers, and they move*
> *towards the dining-room.*
> *The curtain falls.*
> *The curtain rises again at once.*

SCENE II

CHRISTINE, LADY CHESHIRE, DOT, MABEL LANFARNE, *and* JOAN, *are returning to the hall after dinner.*

CHRISTINE. [*in a low voice*] Mother, is it true about young Dunning and Rose Taylor?

LADY CHESHIRE. I'm afraid so, dear.

CHRISTINE. But can't they be——

DOT. Ah! ah-h! [CHRISTINE *and her mother are silent.*] My child, I'm not the young person.

CHRISTINE. No, of course not—only—[*nodding towards* JOAN *and Mabel*].

DOT. Look here! This is just an instance of what I hate.

LADY CHESHIRE. My dear? Another one?

DOT. Yes, mother, and don't you pretend you don't understand, because you know you do.

CHRISTINE. Instance? Of what?

> JOAN *and* MABEL *have ceased talking, and listen,*
> *still at the fire.*

DOT. Humbug, of course. Why should you want them to marry, if he's tired of her?

CHRISTINE. [*Ironically*] Well! If your imagination doesn't carry you as far as that!

DOT. When people marry, do you believe they ought to be in love with each other?

CHRISTINE. [*With a shrug*] That's not the point.

DOT. Oh? Were you in love with Ronny?

CHRISTINE. Don't be idiotic!

DOT. Would you have married him if you hadn't been?

CHRISTINE. Of course not!

JOAN. Dot! You are!——

DOT. Hallo! my little snipe!

LADY CHESHIRE. Dot, dear!

DOT. Don't shut me up, mother! [*To* JOAN.] Are you in love with John? [JOAN *turns hurriedly to the fire.*] Would you be going to marry him if you were not?

CHRISTINE. You are a brute, Dot.

DOT. Is Mabel in love with—whoever she is in love with?

MABEL. And I wonder who that is.

DOT. Well, would you marry him if you weren't?

MABEL. No, I would *not*.

DOT. Now, mother; did you love father?

CHRISTINE. Dot, you really are awful.

DOT. [*Rueful and detached*] Well, it is a bit too thick, perhaps.

JOAN. Dot!

DOT. Well, mother, did you—I mean quite calmly?

LADY CHESHIRE. Yes, dear, quite calmly.

DOT. Would you have married him if you hadn't? [LADY CHESHIRE *shakes her head*] Then we're all agreed!

MABEL. Except yourself.

DOT. [*Grimly*] *Even* if I loved him, he might think himself lucky if I married him.

MABEL. Indeed, and I'm not so sure.

DOT. [*Making a face at her*] What I was going to——

LADY CHESHIRE. But don't you think, dear, you'd better not?

DOT. Well, I won't say what I was going to say, but what I do say is—Why the devil——

LADY CHESHIRE. Quite so, Dot!

DOT. [*A little disconcerted.*] If they're tired of each other, they ought not to marry, and if father's going to make them——

CHRISTINE. You don't understand in the least. It's for the sake of the——

DOT. Out with it, Old Sweetness! The approaching infant! God bless it!

> *There is a sudden silence, for* KEITH *and* LATTER *are seen coming from the dining-room.*

LATTER. That must be so, Ronny.

KEITH. No, John; not a bit of it!

LATTER. You don't *think!*

KEITH. Good Gad, who wants to think after dinner!

DOT. Come on! Let's play pool. [*She turns at the billiard-room door.*] Look here! Rehearsal to-morrow is directly after breakfast; from "Eccles enters breath-less" to the end.

MABEL. Whatever made you choose "Caste," Dot? You know it's awfully difficult.

DOT. Because it's the only play that's not too ad-vanced.   [*The girls all go into the billiard-room.*

LADY CHESHIRE. Where's Bill, Ronny?

KEITH. [*With a grimace*] I rather think Sir William and he are in Committee of Supply—Mem-Sahib.

LADY CHESHIRE. Oh!

> *She looks uneasily at the dining-room; then fol-*
> *lows the girls out.*

LATTER. [*In the tone of one resuming an argument*] There can't be two opinions about it, Ronny. Young Dunning's refusal is simply indefensible.

KEITH. I don't agree a bit, John.

LATTER. Of course, if you won't listen.

KEITH. [*Clipping a cigar*] Draw it mild, my dear chap. We've had the whole thing over twice at least.

LATTER. My point is this——

KEITH. [*Regarding* LATTER *quizzically with his half-closed eyes*] I know—I know—but the point is, how far your point is simply professional.

LATTER. If a man wrongs a woman, he ought to right her again. There's no answer to that.

KEITH. It all depends.

LATTER. That's rank opportunism.

KEITH. Rats! Look here—Oh! hang it, John, one can't argue this out with a parson.

LATTER. [*Frigidly*] Why not?

HAROLD. [*Who has entered from the dining-room*]
Pull devil, pull baker!

KEITH. Shut up, Harold!

LATTER. "To play the game" is the religion even of
the Army.

KEITH. Exactly, but what *is* the game?

LATTER. What else can it be in this case?

KEITH. You're too puritanical, young John. You
can't help it—line of country laid down for you. All
drag-huntin'! What!

LATTER. [*With concentration*] Look here!

HAROLD. [*Imitating the action of a man pulling at a
horse's head*] 'Come hup, I say, you hugly beast!'

KEITH. [*To* LATTER] You're not going to draw me,
old chap. You don't see where you'd land us all. [*He
smokes calmly*]

LATTER. How do you imagine vice takes its rise?
From precisely this sort of thing of young Dunning's.

KEITH. From human nature, I should have thought,
John. I admit that I don't like a fellow's leavin' a girl
in the lurch; but I don't see the use in drawin' hard and
fast rules. You only have to break 'em. Sir William
and you would just tie Dunning and the girl up together,
willy-nilly, to save appearances, and ten to one but
there'll be the deuce to pay in a year's time. You can
take a horse to the water, you can't make him drink.

LATTER. I entirely and absolutely disagree with you.

HAROLD. Good old John!

LATTER. At all events we know where your princi-
ples take you.

KEITH. [*Rather dangerously*] Where, please? [HAROLD *turns up his eyes, and points downwards*] Dry up, Harold!

LATTER. Did you ever hear the story of Faust?

KEITH. Now look here, John; with all due respect to your cloth, and all the politeness in the world, you may go to—blazes.

LATTER. Well, I must say, Ronny—of all the rude boors——   [*He turns towards the billiard-room.*

KEITH. Sorry I smashed the glass, old chap.

> LATTER *passes out. There comes a mingled sound through the opened door, of female voices, laughter, and the click of billiard balls, clipped off by the sudden closing of the door.*

KEITH. [*Impersonally*] Deuced odd, the way a parson puts one's back up! Because you know I agree with him really; young Dunning *ought* to play the game; and I hope Sir William'll make him.

> *The butler* JACKSON *has entered from the door under the stairs followed by the keeper* STUDDENHAM, *a man between fifty and sixty, in a full-skirted coat with big pockets, cord breeches, and gaiters; he has a steady self-respecting weathered face, with blue eyes and a short grey beard, which has obviously once been red.*

KEITH. Hullo! Studdenham!

STUDDENHAM. [*Touching his forehead*] Evenin', Captain Keith.

JACKSON. Sir William still in the dining-room with Mr. Bill, sir?

HAROLD. [*With a grimace*] He is, Jackson.

> JACKSON *goes out to the dining-room.*

KEITH. You've shot no pheasants yet, Studdenham?

STUDDENHAM. No, sir. Only birds. We'll be doin' the spinneys and the home covert while you're down.

KEITH. I say, talkin' of spinneys——

> *He breaks off sharply, and goes out with* HAROLD
> *into the billiard-room.* SIR WILLIAM *enters*
> *from the dining-room, applying a gold tooth-*
> *pick to his front teeth.*

SIR WILLIAM. Ah! Studdenham. Bad business this, about young Dunning!

STUDDENHAM. Yes, Sir William.

SIR WILLIAM. He definitely refuses to marry her?

STUDDENHAM. He does that.

SIR WILLIAM. That won't do, you know. What reason does he give?

STUDDENHAM. Won't say other than that he don't want no more to do with her.

SIR WILLIAM. God bless me! That's not a reason. I can't have a keeper of mine playing fast and loose in the village like this. [*Turning to* LADY CHESHIRE, *who has come in from the billiard-room*] That affair of young Dunning's, my dear.

LADY CHESHIRE. Oh! Yes! I'm *so* sorry, Studdenham. The poor girl!

STUDDENHAM. [*Respectfully*] Fancy he's got a feeling she's not his equal, now, my lady.

LADY CHESHIRE. [*To herself*] Yes, I suppose he *has* made her his superior.

SIR WILLIAM. What? Eh! Quite! Quite! I was just telling Studdenham the fellow must set the matter straight. We can't have open scandals in the village. If he wants to keep his place he must marry her at once.

LADY CHESHIRE. [*To her husband in a low voice*] Is it right to force them? Do you know what the girl wishes, Studdenham?

STUDDENHAM. Shows a spirit, my lady—says she'll have him—willin' or not.

LADY CHESHIRE. A spirit? I see. If they marry like that they're sure to be miserable.

SIR WILLIAM. What! Doesn't follow at all. Besides, my dear, you ought to know by this time, there's an unwritten law in these matters. They're perfectly well aware that when there are consequences, they have to take them.

STUDDENHAM. Some o' these young people, my lady, they don't put two and two together no more than an old cock pheasant.

SIR WILLIAM. I'll give him till to-morrow. If he remains obstinate, he'll have to go; he'll get no character, Studdenham. Let him know what I've said. I like the fellow, he's a good keeper. I don't want to lose him. But this sort of thing I won't have. He must toe the mark or take himself off. Is he up here to-night?

STUDDENHAM. Hangin' partridges, Sir William. Will you have him in?

SIR WILLIAM. [*Hesitating*] Yes—yes. I'll see him.

STUDDENHAM. Good-night to you, my lady.

LADY CHESHIRE. Freda's not looking well, Studdenham.

STUDDENHAM. She's a bit pernickitty with her food, that's where it is.

LADY CHESHIRE. I must try and make her eat.

SIR WILLIAM. Oh! Studdenham. We'll shoot the home covert first. What did we get last year?

STUDDENHAM. [*Producing the game-book; but without reference to it*] Two hundred and fifty-three pheasants, eleven hares, fifty-two rabbits, three woodcock, sundry.

SIR WILLIAM. Sundry? Didn't include a fox did it? [*Gravely*] I was seriously upset this morning at Warnham's spinney——

STUDDENHAM. [*Very gravely*] You don't say, Sir William; that four-year-old he du look a handful!

SIR WILLIAM. [*With a sharp look*] You know well enough what I mean.

STUDDENHAM. [*Unmoved*] Shall I send young Dunning, Sir William?

  SIR WILLIAM *gives a short, sharp nod, and* STUD-
    DENHAM *retires by the door under the stairs.*

SIR WILLIAM. Old fox!

LADY CHESHIRE. Don't be too hard on Dunning. He's very young.

SIR WILLIAM. [*Patting her arm*] My dear, you don't understand young fellows, how should you?

LADY CHESHIRE. [*With her faint irony*] A husband and two sons not counting. [*Then as the door under the stairs is opened*] Bill, now do——

SIR WILLIAM. I'll be gentle with him. [*Sharply*]
Come in!

> LADY CHESHIRE *retires to the billiard-room. She*
> *gives a look back and a half smile at young*
> DUNNING, *a fair young man dressed in brown*
> *cords and leggings, and holding his cap in his*
> *hand; then goes out.*

SIR WILLIAM. Evenin', Dunning.

DUNNING. [*Twisting his cap*] Evenin', Sir William.

SIR WILLIAM. Studdenham's told you what I want
to see you about?

DUNNING. Yes, Sir.

SIR WILLIAM. The thing's in your hands. Take it or
leave it. I don't put pressure on you. I simply won't
have this sort of thing on my estate.

DUNNING. I'd like to say, Sir William, that she—
[*He stops*].

SIR WILLIAM. Yes, I daresay—Six of one and half a
dozen of the other. Can't go into that.

DUNNING. No, Sir William.

SIR WILLIAM. I'm quite mild with you. This is your
first place. If you leave here you'll get no character.

DUNNING. I never meant any harm, sir.

SIR WILLIAM. My good fellow, you know the custom
of the country.

DUNNING. Yes, Sir William, but——

SIR WILLIAM. You should have looked before you
leaped. I'm not forcing you. If you refuse you must
go, that's all.

DUNNING. Yes, Sir William.

SIR WILLIAM. Well, now go along and take a day to think it over.

> BILL, *who has sauntered moodily from the dining-room, stands by the stairs listening. Catching sight of him,* DUNNING *raises his hand to his forelock.*

DUNNING. Very good, Sir William. [*He turns, fumbles, and turns again*] My old mother's dependent on me——

SIR WILLIAM. Now, Dunning, I've no more to say.

> [*Dunning goes sadly away under the stairs.*

SIR WILLIAM. [*Following*] And look here! Just understand this——   [*He too goes out.*

> BILL, *lighting a cigarette, has approached the writing-table. He looks very glum. The billiard-room door is flung open.* MABEL LANFARNE *appears, and makes him a little curtsey.*

MABEL. Against my will I am bidden to bring you in to pool.

BILL. Sorry! I've got letters.

MABEL. You seem to have become very conscientious.

BILL. Oh! I don't know.

MABEL. Do you remember the last day of the covert shooting?

BILL. I do.

MABEL. [*Suddenly*] What a pretty girl Freda Studdenham's grown!

BILL. Has she?

MABEL. "She walks in beauty."

BILL. Really? Hadn't noticed.

MABEL. Have you been taking lessons in conversation?

BILL. Don't think so.

MABEL. Oh! [*There is a silence*] Mr. Cheshire!

BILL. Miss Lanfarne!

MABEL. What's the matter with you? Aren't you rather queer, considering that I don't bite, and *was* rather a pal!

BILL. [*Stolidly*] I'm sorry.

> *Then seeing that his mother has come in from the billiard-room, he sits down at the writing-table.*

LADY CHESHIRE. Mabel, dear, do take my cue. Won't you play too, Bill, and try and stop Ronny, he's too terrible?

BILL. Thanks. I've got these letters.

> MABEL *taking the cue passes back into the billiard-room, whence comes out the sound of talk and laughter.*

LADY CHESHIRE. [*Going over and standing behind her son's chair*] Anything wrong, darling?

BILL. Nothing, thanks. [*Suddenly*] I say, I wish you hadn't asked that girl here.

LADY CHESHIRE. Mabel! Why? She's wanted for rehearsals. I thought you got on so well with her last Christmas.

BILL. [*With a sort of sullen exasperation*] A year ago.

LADY CHESHIRE. The girls like her, so does your father; personally I must say I think she's rather nice and Irish.

BILL. She's all right, I daresay.

He looks round as if to show his mother that he wishes to be left alone. But LADY CHESHIRE, having seen that he is about to look at her, is not looking at him.

LADY CHESHIRE. I'm afraid your father's been talking to you, Bill.

BILL. He has.

LADY CHESHIRE. Debts? Do try and make allowances. [*With a faint smile*] Of course he is a little——

BILL. He is.

LADY CHESHIRE. I wish *I* could——

BILL. Oh, Lord! Don't *you* get mixed up in it!

LADY CHESHIRE. It seems almost a pity that you told him.

BILL. He wrote and asked me point blank what I owed.

LADY CHESHIRE. Oh! [*Forcing herself to speak in a casual voice*] I happen to have a little money, Bill—— I think it would be simpler if——

BILL. Now look here, mother, you've tried that before. I can't help spending money, I never *shall* be able, unless I go to the Colonie , or something of the kind.

LADY CHESHIRE. Don't talk like that, dear!

BILL. I *would*, for two straws!

LADY CHESHIRE. It's only because your father thinks such a lot of the place, and the name, and your career. The Cheshires are all like that. They've been here so long; they're all—root.

BILL. Deuced funny business my career will be, I expect!

LADY CHESHIRE. [*Fluttering, but restraining herself lest he should see*] But, Bill, why *must* you spend more than your allowance?

BILL. Why—anything?   I didn't make myself.

LADY CHESHIRE. I'm afraid *we* did that.   It *was* inconsiderate, perhaps.

BILL. Yes, you'd better have left me out.

LADY CHESHIRE. But why are you so— Only a little fuss about money!

BILL. Ye-es.

LADY CHESHIRE. You're not keeping anything from me, are you?

BILL. [*Facing her*] No. [*He then turns very deliberately to the writing things, and takes up a pen*] I must write these letters, please.

LADY CHESHIRE. Bill, if there's any real trouble, you will tell me, won't you?

BILL. There's nothing whatever.

> *He suddenly gets up and walks about.*
>
> LADY CHESHIRE, *too, moves over to the fireplace, and after an uneasy look at him, turns to the fire.   Then, as if trying to switch off his mood, she changes the subject abruptly.*

LADY CHESHIRE. Isn't it a pity about young Dunning?   I'm so sorry for Rose Taylor.

> *There is a silence.   Stealthily under the staircase* FREDA *has entered, and seeing only* BILL, *advances to speak to him.*

BILL. [*Suddenly*] Oh! well, you can't help these things in the country.

> *As he speaks,* FREDA *stops dead, perceiving that he is not alone;* BILL, *too, catching sight of her, starts.*

LADY CHESHIRE. [*Still speaking to the fire*] It seems dreadful to force him. I do so believe in people doing things of their own accord. [*Then seeing* FREDA *standing so uncertainly by the stairs*] Do you want me, Freda?

FREDA. Only your cloak, my lady. Shall I—begin it?

> *At this moment* SIR WILLIAM *enters from the drawing-room.*

LADY CHESHIRE. Yes, yes.

SIR WILLIAM. [*Genially*] Can you give me another five minutes, Bill? [*Pointing to the billiard-room*] We'll come directly, my dear.

> FREDA, *with a look at* BILL, *has gone back whence she came; and* LADY CHESHIRE *goes reluctantly away into the billiard-room.*

SIR WILLIAM. I shall give young Dunning short shrift. [*He moves over to the fireplace and divides his coat-tails*] Now, about you, Bill! I don't want to bully you the moment you come down, but you know, this can't go on. I've paid your debts twice. Shan't pay them this time unless I see a disposition to change your mode of life. [*A pause*] You get your extravagance from your mother. She's very queer—[*A pause*]—All the Winterleghs are like that about money.

BILL. Mother's particularly generous, if that's what you mean.

SIR WILLIAM. [*Drily*] We will put it that way. [*A pause*] At the present moment you owe, as I understand it, eleven hundred pounds.

BILL. About that.

SIR WILLIAM. Mere flea-bite. [*A pause*] I've a proposition to make.

BILL. Won't it do to-morrow, sir?

SIR WILLIAM. "To-morrow" appears to be your motto in life.

BILL. Thanks!

SIR WILLIAM. I'm anxious to change it to-day. [BILL *looks at him in silence*] It's time you took your position seriously, instead of hanging about town, racing, and playing polo, and what not.

BILL. Go ahead!

At something dangerous in his voice, SIR WILLIAM *modifies his attitude.*

SIR WILLIAM. The proposition's very simple. I can't suppose anything so rational and to your advantage will appeal to you, but [*drily*] I mention it. Marry a nice girl, settle down, and stand for the division; you can have the Dower House and fifteen hundred a year, and I'll pay your debts into the bargain. If you're elected I'll make it two thousand. Plenty of time to work up the constituency before we kick out these infernal Rads. Carpet-bagger against you; if you go hard at it in the summer, it'll be odd if you don't manage to get in your three days a week, next season. You can take Rocketer and that four-year-old—he's well up to your weight, fully eight and a half inches of bone. You'll only want one other. And if Miss—if your wife means to hunt——

BILL. You've chosen my wife, then?

SIR WILLIAM. [*With a quick look*] I imagine, you've some girl in your mind.

BILL. Ah!

SIR WILLIAM. Used not to be unnatural at your age. I married your mother at twenty-eight. Here you are, eldest son of a family that stands for something. The more I see of the times the more I'm convinced that everybody who is anybody has got to buckle to, and save the landmarks left. Unless we're true to our caste, and prepared to work for it, the landed classes are going to go under to this infernal democratic spirit in the air. The outlook's very serious. We're threatened in a hundred ways. If you mean business, you'll want a wife. When I came into the property I should have been lost without your mother.

BILL. I thought this was coming.

SIR WILLIAM. [*With a certain geniality*] My dear fellow, I don't want to put a pistol to your head. You've had a slack rein so far. I've never objected to your sowing a few wild oats—so long as you—er—[*Unseen by* SIR WILLIAM, BILL *makes a sudden movement*] Short of that—at all events, I've not inquired into your affairs. I can only judge by the—er—pecuniary evidence you've been good enough to afford me from time to time. I imagine you've lived like a good many young men in your position—I'm not blaming you, but there's a time for all things.

BILL. Why don't you say outright that you want me to marry Mabel Lanfarne?

SIR WILLIAM. Well, I do. Girl's a nice one. Good family—got a little money—rides well. Isn't she good-looking enough for you, or what?

BILL. Quite, thanks.

SIR WILLIAM. I understood from your mother that you and she were on good terms.

BILL. Please don't drag mother into it.

SIR WILLIAM. [*With dangerous politeness*] Perhaps you'll be good enough to state your objections.

BILL. Must we go on with this?

SIR WILLIAM. I've never asked you to do anything for me before; I expect you to pay attention now. I've no wish to dragoon you into this particular marriage. If you don't care for Miss Lanfarne, marry a girl you're fond of.

BILL. I refuse.

SIR WILLIAM. In that case you know what to look out for. [*With a sudden rush of choler*] You young . . . [*He checks himself and stands glaring at* BILL, *who glares back at him*] This means, I suppose, that you've got some entanglement or other.

BILL. Suppose what you like, sir.

SIR WILLIAM. I warn you, if you play the black-guard——

BILL. You can't force me like young Dunning.

> *Hearing the raised voices* LADY CHESHIRE *has come back from the billiard-room.*

LADY CHESHIRE. [*Closing the door*] What is it?

SIR WILLIAM. You deliberately refuse! Go away, Dorothy.

LADY CHESHIRE. [*Resolutely*] I haven't seen Bill for two months.

SIR WILLIAM. What! [*Hesitating*] Well—we must talk it over again.

LADY CHESHIRE. Come to the billiard-room, both of you! Bill, *do* finish those letters!

> *With a deft movement she draws* SIR WILLIAM *toward the billiard-room, and glances back at* BILL *before going out, but he has turned to the writing-table. When the door is closed,* BILL *looks into the drawing-room, then opens the door under the stairs; and backing away towards the writing-table, sits down there, and takes up a pen.* FREDA *who has evidently been waiting, comes in and stands by the table.*

BILL. I say, this is dangerous, you know.

FREDA. Yes—but I must.

BILL. Well, then—[*With natural recklessness*] Aren't you going to kiss me?

> *Without moving she looks at him with a sort of miserable inquiry.*

BILL. Do you know you haven't seen me for eight weeks?

FREDA. Quite—long enough—for you to have forgotten.

BILL. Forgotten! I don't forget people so soon.

FREDA. No?

BILL. What's the matter with you, Freda?

FREDA. [*After a long look*] It'll never be as it was.

BILL. [*Jumping up*] How d'you mean?

FREDA. I've got something for you. [*She takes a diamond ring out of her dress and holds it out to him*] I've not worn it since Cromer.

BILL. Now, look here——

FREDA. I've had my holiday; I shan't get another in a hurry.

BILL. Freda!

FREDA. You'll be glad to be free. That fortnight's all you really loved me in.

BILL. [*Putting his hands on her arms*] I swear——

FREDA. [*Between her teeth*] Miss Lanfarne need never know about me.

BILL. So that's it! I've told you a dozen times—nothing's changed.   [FREDA *looks at him and smiles.*

BILL. Oh! very well! If you *will* make yourself miserable.

FREDA. Everybody will be pleased.

BILL. At what?

FREDA. When you marry her.

BILL. This is too bad.

FREDA. It's what always happens—even when it's not a gentleman.

BILL. That's enough.

FREDA. But I'm not like that girl down in the village. You needn't be afraid I'll say anything when—it comes. That's what I had to tell you.

BILL. *What!*

FREDA. *I* can keep a secret.

BILL. Do you mean this?   [*She bows her head.*

BILL. Good God!

FREDA. Father brought me up not to whine.   Like the puppies when they hold them up by their tails. [*With a sudden break in her voice*] Oh! Bill!

BILL. [*With his head down, seizing her hands*] Freda! [*He breaks away from her towards the fire*] Good God!

> *She stands looking at him, then quietly slips away by the door under the staircase.* BILL *turns to speak to her, and sees that she has gone. He walks up to the fireplace, and grips the mantelpiece.*

BILL. By Jove!   This is ——!

The curtain falls.

ACT II

The scene is LADY CHESHIRE'S *morning room, at ten
o'clock on the following day. It is a pretty room,
with white panelled walls; and chrysanthemums and
carmine lilies in bowls. A large bow window over-
looks the park under a sou'-westerly sky. A piano
stands open; a fire is burning; and the morning's
correspondence is scattered on a writing-table. Doors
opposite each other lead to the maid's workroom, and
to a corridor.* LADY CHESHIRE *is standing in the
middle of the room, looking at an opera cloak, which*
FREDA *is holding out.*

LADY CHESHIRE. Well, Freda, suppose you just give
it up!

FREDA. I don't like to be beaten.

LADY CHESHIRE. You're not to worry over your
work. And by the way, I promised your father to
make you eat more.   [FREDA *smiles.*

LADY CHESHIRE. It's all very well to smile. You
want bracing up. Now don't be naughty. I shall
give you a tonic. And I think you had better put that
cloak away.

FREDA. I'd rather have one more try, my lady.

LADY CHESHIRE. [*Sitting down at her writing-table*]
Very well.

    FREDA *goes out into her workroom, as* JACKSON
    comes in from the corridor.

JACKSON. Excuse me, my lady. There's a young woman from the village, says you wanted to see her.

LADY CHESHIRE. Rose Taylor? Ask her to come in. Oh! and Jackson the car for the meet please at half-past ten.

> JACKSON *having bowed and withdrawn,* LADY CHESHIRE *rises with marked signs of nervousness, which she has only just suppressed, when* ROSE TAYLOR, *a stolid country girl, comes in and stands waiting by the door.*

LADY CHESHIRE. Well, Rose. Do come in!

[ROSE *advances perhaps a couple of steps.*

LADY CHESHIRE. I just wondered whether you'd like to ask my advice. Your engagement with Dunning's broken off, isn't it?

ROSE. Yes—but I've told him he's got to marry me.

LADY CHESHIRE. I see! And you think that'll be the wisest thing?

ROSE. [*Stolidly*] I don't know, my lady. He's *got* to.

LADY CHESHIRE. I do hope you're a little fond of him still.

ROSE. I'm *not*. He don't deserve it.

LADY CHESHIRE. And—do you think he's quite lost his affection for you?

ROSE. I suppose so, else he wouldn't treat me as he's done. He's after that—that—He didn't ought to treat me as if I was dead.

LADY CHESHIRE. No, no—of course. But you *will* think it all well over, won't you?

ROSE. I've a-got nothing to think over, except what I know of.

LADY CHESHIRE. But for you both to marry in that spirit! You know it's for life, Rose. [*Looking into her face*] I'm always ready to help you.

ROSE. [*Dropping a very slight curtsey*] Thank you, my lady, but I think he ought to marry me. I've told him he ought.

LADY CHESHIRE. [*Sighing*] Well, that's all I wanted to say. It's a question of your self-respect; I can't give you any real advice. But just remember that if you want a friend——

ROSE. [*With a gulp*] I'm not so 'ard, really. I only want him to do what's right by me.

LADY CHESHIRE. [*With a little lift of her eyebrows— gently*] Yes, yes—I see.

ROSE. [*Glancing back at the door*] I don't like meeting the servants.

LADY CHESHIRE. Come along, I'll take you out another way. [*As they reach the door,* DOT *comes in.*

DOT. [*With a glance at* ROSE] Can we have this room for the mouldy rehearsal, Mother?

LADY CHESHIRE. Yes, dear, you can air it here.

> *Holding the door open for* ROSE *she follows her out. And* DOT, *with a book of "Caste" in her hand, arranges the room according to a diagram.*

DOT. Chair—chair—table—chair—Dash! Table— piano—fire—window! [*Producing a pocket comb*] Comb for Eccles. Cradle?—Cradle—[*She viciously dumps a*

waste-paper basket down, and drops a footstool into it]
Brat! [*Then reading from the book gloomily*] "Enter
Eccles breathless. Esther and Polly rise—Esther puts
on lid of bandbox." Bandbox!

    Searching for something to represent a bandbox,
    she opens the workroom door.

DOT. Freda?

      FREDA *comes in.*

DOT. I say, Freda. Anything the matter? You
seem awfully down.   [FREDA *does not answer.*

DOT. You haven't looked anything of a lollipop
lately.

FREDA. I'm quite all right, thank you, Miss Dot.

DOT. Has Mother been givin' you a tonic?

FREDA. [*Smiling a little*] Not yet.

DOT. That doesn't account for it then. [*With a
sudden warm impulse*] What *is* it, Freda?

FREDA. Nothing.

DOT. [*Switching off on a different line of thought*]
Are you very busy this morning?

FREDA. Only this cloak for my lady.

DOT. Oh! that can wait. I may have to get you in
to prompt, if I can't keep 'em straight. [*Gloomily*] They
stray so. Would you mind?

FREDA. [*Stolidly*] I shall be very glad, Miss Dot.

DOT. [*Eyeing her dubiously*] All right. Let's see—
what did I want?

      JOAN *has come in.*

JOAN. Look here, Dot; about the baby in this scene.
I'm sure I ought to make more of it.

DOT. Romantic little beast! [*She plucks the footstool out by one ear, and holds it forth*] Let's see you try!

JOAN. [*Recoiling*] But, Dot, what are we really going to have for the baby? I can't rehearse with that thing. Can't *you* suggest something, Freda?

FREDA. Borrow a real one, Miss Joan. There are some that don't count much.

JOAN. Freda, how horrible!

DOT. [*Dropping the footstool back into the basket*] You'll just put up with what you're given.

> Then as CHRISTINE and MABEL LANFARNE *come in,* FREDA *turns abruptly and goes out.*

DOT. Buck up! Where are Bill and Harold? [*To* JOAN] Go and find them, mouse-cat.

> But BILL *and* HAROLD, *followed by* LATTER, *are already in the doorway. They come in, and* LATTER, *stumbling over the waste-paper basket, takes it up to improve its position.*

DOT. Drop that cradle, John! [*As he picks the footstool out of it*] Leave the baby in! Now then! Bill, you enter there! [*She points to the workroom door where* BILL *and* MABEL *range themselves close to the piano; while* HAROLD *goes to the window*] John! get off the stage! Now then, "Eccles enters breathless, Esther and Polly rise." Wait a minute. I know now. [*She opens the workroom door*] Freda, I wanted a band-box.

HAROLD. [*Cheerfully*] I hate beginning to rehearse, you know, you feel such a fool.

DOT. [*With her bandbox—gloomily*] You'll feel more of a fool when you have begun. [*To* BILL, *who is staring into the workroom*] Shut the door. Now.

[BILL *shuts the door.*

LATTER. [*Advancing*] Look here! I want to clear up a point of psychology before we start.

DOT. Good Lord!

LATTER. When I bring in the milk—ought I to bring it in seriously—as if I were accustomed—I mean, I maintain that if I'm——

JOAN. Oh! John, but I don't think it's meant that you should——

DOT. Shut up! Go back, John! Blow the milk! Begin, begin, begin! Bill!

LATTER. [*Turning round and again advancing*] But I think you underrate the importance of my entrance altogether.

MABEL. Oh! no, Mr. Latter!

LATTER. I don't in the least want to destroy the balance of the scene, but I do want to be clear about the spirit. What is the spirit?

DOT. [*With gloom*] Rollicking!

LATTER. Well, I don't think so. We shall run a great risk with this play, if we rollick.

DOT. Shall we? Now look here——!

MABEL. [*Softly to* BILL] Mr. Cheshire!

BILL. [*Desperately*] Let's get on!

DOT. [*Waving* LATTER *back*] Begin, begin! At last!

But JACKSON *has come in.*

JACKSON. [*To* CHRISTINE] Studdenham says, M'm, if the young ladies want to see the spaniel pups, he's brought 'em round.

JOAN. [*Starting up*] Oh! come on, John!

[*She flies towards the door, followed by* LATTER.

DOT. [*Gesticulating with her book*] Stop! You——

[CHRISTINE *and* HAROLD *also rush past.*

DOT. [*Despairingly*] First pick! [*Tearing her hair*] Pigs! Devils!   [*She rushes after them.*

BILL *and* MABEL *are left alone.*

MABEL. [*Mockingly*] And don't *you* want one of the spaniel pups?

BILL. [*Painfully reserved and sullen, and conscious of the workroom door*] Can't keep a dog in town. You can have one, if you like. The breeding's all right.

MABEL. Sixth pick?

BILL. The girls'll give you one of theirs. They only fancy they want 'em.

MABEL. [*Moving nearer to him, with her hands clasped behind her*] You know, you remind me awfully of your father. Except that you're not nearly so polite. I don't understand you English—lords of the soil. The way you have of disposing of your females. [*With a sudden change of voice*] What was the matter with you last night? [*Softly*] Won't you tell me?

BILL. Nothing to tell.

MABEL. Ah! no, Mr. Bill.

BILL. [*Almost succumbing to her voice—then sullenly*] Worried, I suppose.

MABEL. [*Returning to her mocking*] Quite got over it?

BILL. Don't chaff me, please.

MABEL. You really are rather formidable.

BILL. Thanks.

MABEL. But, you know, I love to cross a field where there's a bull.

BILL. Really! Very interesting.

MABEL. The way of their only seeing one thing at a time. [*She moves back as he advances*] And overturning people on the journey.

BILL. Hadn't you better be a little careful?

MABEL. And never to see the hedge until they're stuck in it. And then straight from that hedge into the opposite one.

BILL. [*Savagely*] What makes you bait me this morning of all mornings?

MABEL. The beautiful morning! [*Suddenly*] It must be dull for poor Freda working in there with all this fun going on?

BILL. [*Glancing at the door*] Fun you call it?

MABEL. To go back to you, now—Mr. Cheshire.

BILL. No.

MABEL. You always make me feel so Irish. Is it because you're so English, d'you think? Ah! I can see him moving his ears. Now he's pawing the ground— He's started!

BILL. Miss Lanfarne!

MABEL. [*Still backing away from him, and drawing him on with her eyes and smile*] You can't help coming

after me! [*Then with a sudden change to a sort of stern
gravity*] Can you? You'll feel that when I've gone.

> *They stand quite still, looking into each other's
> eyes and* FREDA, *who has opened the door of
> the workroom stares at them.*

MABEL. [*Seeing her*] Here's the stile. *Adieu, Mon-
sieur le taureau!*

> *She puts her hand behind her, opens the door, and
> slips through, leaving* BILL *to turn, following
> the direction of her eyes, and see* FREDA *with
> the cloak still in her hand.*

BILL. [*Slowly walking towards her*] I haven't slept
all night.

FREDA. No?

BILL. Have you been thinking it over?

> [FREDA *gives a bitter little laugh.*

BILL. Don't! We must make a plan. I'll get you
away. I won't let you suffer. I swear I won't.

FREDA. That will be clever.

BILL. I wish to Heaven my affairs weren't in such a
mess.

FREDA. I shall be—all—right, thank you.

BILL. You *must* think me a blackguard. [*She shakes
her head*] Abuse me—say something! Don't look like
that!

FREDA. Were you ever really fond of me?

BILL. Of course I was, I am now. Give me your
hands.

> *She looks at him, then drags her hands from his,
> and covers her face.*

BILL. [*Clenching his fists*] Look here! I'll prove it.
[*Then as she suddenly flings her arms round his neck and
clings to him*] There, there!

> *There is a click of a door handle.   They start away
> from each other, and see* LADY CHESHIRE *re-
> garding them.*

LADY CHESHIRE. [*Without irony*] I beg your pardon.

> *She makes as if to withdraw from an unwarranted
> intrusion, but suddenly turning, stands, with
> lips pressed together, waiting.*

LADY CHESHIRE. Yes?

> FREDA *has muffled her face.   But* BILL *turns and
> confronts his mother.*

BILL. Don't say anything against her!

LADY CHESHIRE. [*Tries to speak to him and fails—
then to* FREDA] Please—go!

BILL. [*Taking* FREDA's *arm*] No.

> LADY CHESHIRE, *after a moment's hesitation, her-
> self moves towards the door.*

BILL. Stop, mother!

LADY CHESHIRE. I think perhaps not.

BILL. [*Looking at* FREDA, *who is cowering as though
from a blow*] It's a d—d shame!

LADY CHESHIRE. It is.

BILL. [*With sudden resolution*] It's not as you think.
I'm engaged to be married to her.

> [FREDA *gives him a wild stare, and turns away.*

LADY CHESHIRE. [*Looking from one to the other*] I—
don't—think—I—quite—understand.

BILL. [*With the brutality of his mortification*] What I said was plain enough.

LADY CHESHIRE. Bill!

BILL. I tell you I am going to marry her.

LADY CHESHIRE. [*To* FREDA] Is that true?

> [FREDA *gulps and remains silent.*

BILL. If you want to say anything, say it to *me*, mother.

LADY CHESHIRE. [*Gripping the edge of a little table*] Give me a chair, please.   [BILL *gives her a chair.*

LADY CHESHIRE. [*To* FREDA] Please sit down too.

> FREDA *sits on the piano stool, still turning her face away.*

LADY CHESHIRE. [*Fixing her eyes on* FREDA] Now!

BILL. I fell in love with her. And she with me.

LADY CHESHIRE. When?

BILL. In the summer.

LADY CHESHIRE. Ah!

BILL. It wasn't her fault.

LADY CHESHIRE. No?

BILL. [*With a sort of menace*] Mother!

LADY CHESHIRE. Forgive me, I am not quite used to the idea. You say that you—are engaged?

BILL. Yes.

LADY CHESHIRE. The reasons against such an engagement have occurred to you, I suppose? [*With a sudden change of tone*] Bill! what does it mean?

BILL. If you think she's trapped me into this——

LADY CHESHIRE. I do not.   Neither do I think she has been trapped. I think nothing. I understand nothing.

BILL. [*Grimly*] Good!

LADY CHESHIRE. How long has this—engagement lasted?

BILL. [*After a silence*] Two months.

LADY CHESHIRE. [*Suddenly*] This is—this is quite impossible.

BILL. You'll find it isn't.

LADY CHESHIRE. It's simple misery.

BILL. [*Pointing to the workroom*] Go and wait in there, Freda.

LADY CHESHIRE. [*Quickly*] And are you still in love with her?

> FREDA, *moving towards the workroom, smothers a sob.*

BILL. Of course I am.

> FREDA *has gone, and as she goes,* LADY CHESHIRE *rises suddenly, forced by the intense feeling she has been keeping in hand.*

LADY CHESHIRE. Bill! Oh, Bill! What does it all mean? [BILL, *looking from side to side, only shrugs his shoulders*] You are *not* in love with her now. It's no good telling me you are.

BILL. I am.

LADY CHESHIRE. That's not exactly how you would speak if you were.

BILL. She's in love with me.

LADY CHESHIRE. [*Bitterly*] I suppose so.

BILL. I mean to see that nobody runs her down.

LADY CHESHIRE. [*With difficulty*] Bill! Am I a hard, or mean woman?

BILL. Mother!

LADY CHESHIRE. It's all your life—and—your father's—and—all of us. I want to understand—I must understand. Have you realised what an awful thing this would be for us all? It's quite impossible that it should go on.

BILL. I'm always in hot water with the Governor, as it is. She and I'll take good care not to be in the way.

LADY CHESHIRE. Tell me everything!

BILL. I have.

LADY CHESHIRE. I'm your mother, Bill.

BILL. What's the good of these questions?

LADY CHESHIRE. You won't give her away—I see!

BILL. I've told you all there is to tell. We're engaged, we shall be married quietly, and—and—go to Canada.

LADY CHESHIRE. If there weren't more than that to tell you'd be in love with her now.

BILL. I've told you that I am.

LADY CHESHIRE. You are *not*. [*Almost fiercely*] I *know*—I *know* there's more behind.

BILL. There—is—nothing.

LADY CHESHIRE. [*Baffled, but unconvinced*] Do you mean that your love for her has been just what it might have been for a lady?

BILL. [*Bitterly*] Why not?

LADY CHESHIRE. [*With painful irony*] It is not so as a rule.

BILL. Up to now I've never heard you or the girls say a word against Freda. This isn't the moment to begin, please.

LADY CHESHIRE. [*Solemnly*] All such marriages end in wretchedness. You haven't a taste or tradition in common. You don't know what marriage is. Day after day, year after year. It's no use being sentimental—for people brought up as we are to have different manners is worse than to have different souls. Besides, it's poverty. Your father will never forgive you, and *I've* practically nothing. What can you do? You have no profession. How are you going to stand it; with a woman who——? It's the little things.

BILL. I know all that, thanks.

LADY CHESHIRE. Nobody does till they've been through it. Marriage is hard enough when people are of the same class. [*With a sudden movement towards him*] Oh! my dear—before it's too late!

BILL. [*After a struggle*] It's no good.

LADY CHESHIRE. It's not fair to her. It *can* only end in her misery.

BILL. Leave that to me, please.

LADY CHESHIRE. [*With an almost angry vehemence*] Only the very finest can do such things. And you— don't even know what trouble's like.

BILL. Drop it, please, mother.

LADY CHESHIRE. Bill, on your word of honour, are you acting of your own free will?

BILL. [*Breaking away from her*] I can't stand any more.   [*He goes out into the workroom.*

LADY CHESHIRE. What in God's name shall I do?

In her distress she walks up and down the room, then goes to the workroom door, and opens it.

LADY CHESHIRE. Come in here, please, Freda.

After a second's pause, FREDA, *white and trembling, appears in the doorway, followed by* BILL.

LADY CHESHIRE. No, Bill. I want to speak to her alone.

BILL *does not move.*

LADY CHESHIRE. [*Icily*] I must ask you to leave us.

BILL *hesitates; then shrugging his shoulders, he touches* FREDA'S *arms, and goes back into the workroom, closing the door. There is silence.*

LADY CHESHIRE. How did it come about?

FREDA. I don't know, my lady.

LADY CHESHIRE. For heaven's sake, child, don't call me that again, whatever happens. [*She walks to the window, and speaks from there*] I know well enough how love comes. I don't blame you. Don't cry. But, you see, it's my eldest son. [FREDA *puts her hand to her breast*] Yes, I know. Women always get the worst of these things. That's natural. But it's not only you— is it? Does any one guess?

FREDA. No.

LADY CHESHIRE. Not even your father? [FREDA *shakes her head*] There's nothing more dreadful than for a woman to hang like a stone round a man's neck. How far has it gone? Tell me!

FREDA. I can't.

LADY CHESHIRE. Come!

FREDA. I—won't.

LADY CHESHIRE. [*Smiling painfully*]. Won't give him away? Both of you the same. What's the use of that with me? Look at me! Wasn't he with you when you went for your holiday this summer?

FREDA. He's—always—behaved—like—a—gentleman.

LADY CHESHIRE. Like a *man*—you mean!

FREDA. It hasn't been his fault! I love him so.

> LADY CHESHIRE *turns abruptly, and begins to walk up and down the room. Then stopping, she looks intently at* FREDA.

LADY CHESHIRE. I don't know what to say to you. It's simple madness! It can't, and shan't go on.

FREDA. [*Sullenly*] I know I'm not his equal, but I am—somebody.

LADY CHESHIRE. [*Answering this first assertion of rights with a sudden steeliness*] Does he love you *now?*

FREDA. That's not fair—it's not fair.

LADY CHESHIRE. If men are like gunpowder, Freda, women are not. If you've lost him it's been your own fault.

FREDA. But he *does* love me, he must. It's only four months.

LADY CHESHIRE. [*Looking down, and speaking rapidly*] Listen to me. I love my son, but I know him—I know all his kind of man. I've lived with one for thirty years. I know the way their senses work. When they want a thing they must have it, and then—they're sorry.

FREDA. [*Sullenly*] He's *not* sorry.

LADY CHESHIRE. Is his love big enough to carry you both over everything? . . . You know it isn't.

FREDA. If I were a lady, you wouldn't talk like that.

LADY CHESHIRE. If you were a lady there'd be no trouble before either of you. You'll make him hate you.

FREDA. I won't believe it. I could make him happy —out there.

LADY CHESHIRE. I don't want to be so odious as to say all the things you must know. I only ask you to try and put yourself in our position.

FREDA. Ah, yes!

LADY CHESHIRE. You ought to know me better than to think I'm purely selfish.

FREDA. Would you like to put yourself in my position? [*She throws up her head.*

LADY CHESHIRE. What!

FREDA. Yes. Just like Rose.

LADY CHESHIRE. [*In a low, horror-stricken voice*] Oh!
          *There is a dead silence, then going swiftly up to
          her, she looks straight into* FREDA's *eyes.*

FREDA. [*Meeting her gaze*] Oh! Yes—it's the truth. [*Then to Bill who has come in from the workroom, she gasps out*] I never meant to tell.

BILL. Well, are you satisfied?

LADY CHESHIRE. [*Below her breath*] This is terrible!

BILL. The Governor had better know.

LADY CHESHIRE. Oh! no; not yet!

BILL. Waiting won't cure it!

> *The door from the corridor is thrown open;* CHRIS-
> TINE *and* DOT *run in with their copies of the
> play in their hands; seeing that something is
> wrong, they stand still. After a look at his
> mother,* BILL *turns abruptly, and goes back into
> the workroom.* LADY CHESHIRE *moves towards
> the window.*

JOAN. [*Following her sisters*] The car's round.
What's the matter?

DOT. Shut up!

> SIR WILLIAM'S *voice is heard from the corridor
> calling "Dorothy!" As* LADY CHESHIRE, *pass-
> ing her handkerchief over her face, turns round,
> he enters. He is in full hunting dress: well-
> weathered pink, buckskins, and mahogany tops.*

SIR WILLIAM. Just off, my dear. [*To his daughters,
genially*] Rehearsin'? What! [*He goes up to* FREDA
holding out his gloved right hand] Button that for me,
Freda, would you? It's a bit stiff!

> FREDA *buttons the glove:* LADY CHESHIRE *and
> the girls watching in hypnotic silence.*

SIR WILLIAM. Thank you! "Balmy as May"; scent
ought to be first-rate. [*To* LADY CHESHIRE] Good-bye,
my dear! Sampson's Gorse—best day of the whole
year. [*He pats* JOAN *on the shoulder*] Wish you were
comin' out, Joan.

> *He goes out, leaving the door open, and as his
> footsteps and the chink of his spurs die away,*
> FREDA *turns and rushes into the workroom.*

CHRISTINE. Mother! What——?

> *But* LADY CHESHIRE *waves the question aside,*
> *passes her daughter, and goes out into the cor-*
> *ridor. The sound of a motor car is heard.*

JOAN. [*Running to the window*] They've started—!
—Chris! What is it? Dot?

DOT. Bill, and her!

JOAN. But *what?*

DOT. [*Gloomily*] Heaven knows! Go away, you're
not fit for this.

JOAN. [*Aghast*] I am fit.

DOT. I think not.

JOAN. Chris?

CHRISTINE. [*In a hard voice*] Mother ought to have
told us.

JOAN. It can't be very awful. Freda's so *good.*

DOT. Call yourself in love, you milk-and-water—
kitten!

CHRISTINE. It's horrible, not knowing anything! I
wish Ronny hadn't gone.

JOAN. Shall I fetch John?

DOT. John!

CHRISTINE. Perhaps Harold knows.

JOAN. He went out with Studdenham.

DOT. It's always like this, women kept in blinkers.
Rose-leaves and humbug! That awful old man!

JOAN. Dot!

CHRISTINE. Don't talk of father like that!

DOT. Well, he is! And Bill will be just like him at
fifty! Heaven help Freda, whatever she's done! I'd

sooner be a private in a German regiment than a woman.

JOAN. Dot, you're awful.

DOT. You—mouse-hearted—linnet!

CHRISTINE. Don't talk that nonsense about women!

DOT. You're married and out of it; and Ronny's not one of these terrific John Bulls. [*To* JOAN *who has opened the door*] Looking for John? No good, my dear; lath and plaster.

JOAN. [*From the door, in a frightened whisper*] Here's Mabel!

DOT. Heavens, and the waters under the earth!

CHRISTINE. If we only *knew!*

> *As* MABEL *comes in, the three girls are silent, with their eyes fixed on their books.*

MABEL. The silent company.

DOT. [*Looking straight at her*] We're chucking it for to-day.

MABEL. What's the matter?

CHRISTINE. Oh! nothing.

DOT. Something's happened.

MABEL. Really! I *am* sorry. [*Hesitating*] Is it bad enough for me to go?

CHRISTINE. Oh! no, Mabel!

DOT. [*Sardonically*] I should think very likely.

> *While she is looking from face to face,* BILL *comes in from the workroom. He starts to walk across the room, but stops, and looks stolidly at the four girls.*

BILL. Exactly! Fact of the matter is, Miss Lanfarne, I'm engaged to my mother's maid.

> *No one moves or speaks. Suddenly* MABEL
> LANFARNE *goes towards him, holding out her
> hand.* BILL *does not take her hand, but bows.
> Then after a swift glance at the girls' faces*
> MABEL *goes out into the corridor, and the three
> girls are left staring at their brother.*

BILL. [*Coolly*] Thought you might like to know.

> [*He, too, goes out into the corridor.*

CHRISTINE. Great heavens!

JOAN. How *awful!*

CHRISTINE. I never thought of anything as bad as that.

JOAN. Oh! Chris! Something must be done!

DOT. [*Suddenly to herself*] Ha! When Father went up
to have his glove buttoned!

> *There is a sound,* JACKSON *has come in from the
> corridor.*

JACKSON. [*To* DOT] If you please, Miss, Studdenham's brought up the other two pups. He's just out-
side. Will you kindly take a look at them, he says?

> *There is silence.*

DOT. [*Suddenly*] We can't.

CHRISTINE. Not just now, Jackson.

JACKSON. Is Studdenham and the pups to wait, M'm?

> DOT *shakes her head violently. But* STUDDEN-
> HAM *is seen already standing in the doorway,
> with a spaniel puppy in either side-pocket. He
> comes in, and* JACKSON *stands waiting behind
> him.*

STUDDENHAM. This fellow's the best, Miss Dot. [*He protrudes the right-hand pocket*] I was keeping him for my girl—a proper breedy one—takes after his father.

The girls stare at him in silence.

DOT. [*Hastily*] Thanks, Studdenham, I see.

STUDDENHAM. I won't take 'em out in here. They're rather bold yet.

CHRISTINE. [*Desperately*] No, no, of course.

STUDDENHAM. Then you think you'd like him, Miss Dot? The other's got a white chest; she's a lady.

[*He protrudes the left-hand pocket.*

DOT. Oh, yes! Studdenham; thanks, thanks awfully.

STUDDENHAM. Wonderful faithful creatures; follow you like a woman. You can't shake 'em off anyhow. [*He protrudes the right-hand pocket*] My girl, she'd set her heart on *him*, but she'll just have to do without.

DOT. [*As though galvanised*] Oh! no, I can't take it away from *her*.

STUDDENHAM. Bless you, she won't mind! That's settled, then. [*He turns to the door. To the* PUPPY] Ah! would you! Tryin' to wriggle out of it! Regular young limb!   [*He goes out, followed by* JACKSON.

CHRISTINE. How ghastly!

DOT. [*Suddenly catching sight of the book in her hand*] "Caste!"   [*She gives vent to a short sharp laugh.*

The curtain falls.

ACT III

It is five o'clock of the same day. The scene is the smoking-room, with walls of Leander red, covered by old steeplechase and hunting prints. Armchairs encircle a high-fendered hearth, in which a fire is burning. The curtains are not yet drawn across mullioned windows; but electric light is burning. There are two doors, leading, the one to the billiard-room, the other to a corridor. BILL is pacing up and down; HAROLD, at the fireplace, stands looking at him with commiseration.

BILL. What's the time?

HAROLD. Nearly five. They won't be in yet, if that's any consolation. Always a tough meet—[*softly*] as the tiger said when he ate the man.

BILL. By Jove! You're the only person I can stand within a mile of me, Harold.

HAROLD. Old boy! Do you seriously think you're going to make it any better by marrying her?

[*Bill shrugs his shoulders, still pacing the room.*

BILL. Look here! I'm not the sort that finds it easy to say things.

HAROLD. No, old man.

BILL. But I've got a kind of self-respect though you wouldn't think it!

HAROLD. My dear old chap!

53

BILL. This is about as low-down a thing as one could have done, I suppose—one's own mother's maid; we've known her since she was so high. I see it now that— I've got over the attack.

HAROLD. But, heavens! if you're no longer keen on her, Bill! Do apply your reason, old boy.

There is silence; while BILL *again paces up and down.*

BILL. If you think I care two straws about the morality of the thing——

HAROLD. Oh! my dear old man! Of course not!

BILL. It's simply that I shall feel such a d—d skunk, if I leave her in the lurch, with everybody knowing. Try it yourself; you'd soon see!

HAROLD. Poor old chap!

BILL. It's not as if she'd tried to force me into it. And she's a soft little thing. Why I ever made such a sickening ass of myself, I can't think. I never meant—

HAROLD. No, I know! But, don't do anything rash, Bill; keep your head, old man!

BILL. I don't see what loss I should be, if I did clear out of the country. [*The sound of cannoning billiard balls is heard*] Who's that knocking the balls about?

HAROLD. John, I expect.   [*The sound ceases.*

BILL. He's coming in here. Can't stand that!

As LATTER *appears from the billiard-room, he goes hurriedly out.*

LATTER. Was that Bill?

HAROLD. Yes.

LATTER. Well?

HAROLD. [*Pacing up and down in his turn*] Rat in a cage is a fool to him. This is the sort of thing you read of in books, John! What price your argument with Ronny now? Well, it's not too late for *you* luckily.

LATTER. What do you mean?

HAROLD. You needn't connect yourself with this eccentric family!

LATTER. I'm not a bounder, Harold.

HAROLD. Good!

LATTER. It's terrible for your sisters.

HAROLD. Deuced lucky we haven't a lot of people staying here! Poor mother! John, I feel awfully bad about this. If something isn't done, pretty mess I shall be in.

LATTER. How?

HAROLD. There's no entail. If the Governor cuts Bill off, it'll all come to me.

LATTER. Oh!

HAROLD. Poor old Bill! I say, the play! Nemesis! What? Moral! Caste don't matter. Got us fairly on the hop.

LATTER. It's too bad of Bill. It really is. He's behaved disgracefully.

HAROLD. [*Warmly*] Well! There are thousands of fellows who'd never dream of sticking to the girl, considering what it means.

LATTER. Perfectly disgusting!

HAROLD. Hang you, John! Haven't you any human sympathy? Don't you know how these things come about? It's like a spark in a straw-yard.

LATTER. One doesn't take lighted pipes into straw-yards unless one's an idiot, or worse.

HAROLD. H'm! [*With a grin*] You're not allowed to-bacco. In the good old days no one would have thought anything of this. My great-grandfather——

LATTER. Spare me your great-grandfather.

HAROLD. I could tell you of at least a dozen men I know who've been through this same business, and got off scot-free; and now because Bill's going to play the game, it'll smash him up.

LATTER. Why didn't he play the game at the begin-ning?

HAROLD. I can't stand your sort, John. When a thing like this happens, all you can do is to cry out: Why didn't he—? Why didn't she—? What's to be *done*—that's the point!

LATTER. Of course he'll have to——

HAROLD. Ha!

LATTER. What do you mean by—that?

HAROLD. Look here, John! You feel in your bones that a marriage'll be hopeless, just as I do, knowing Bill and the girl and everything! Now don't you?

LATTER. The whole thing is—is most unfortunate.

HAROLD. By Jove! I should think it was!

> *As he speaks* CHRISTINE *and* KEITH *come in from the billiard-room. He is still in splashed hunting clothes, and looks exceptionally weath-ered, thin-lipped, reticent. He lights a cigarette and sinks into an armchair. Behind them* DOT *and* JOAN *have come stealing in.*

CHRISTINE. I've told Ronny.

JOAN. This waiting for father to be told is awful.

HAROLD. [*To* KEITH] Where did you leave the old man?

KEITH. Clackenham. He'll be home in ten minutes.

DOT. Mabel's going. [*They all stir, as if at fresh consciousness of discomfiture*]. She walked into Gracely and sent herself a telegram.

HAROLD. Phew!

DOT. And we shall say good-bye, as if nothing had happened!

HAROLD. It's up to you, Ronny.

> KEITH, *looking at* JOAN, *slowly emits smoke; and* LATTER *passing his arm through* JOAN's, *draws her away with him into the billiard-room.*

KEITH. Dot?

DOT. *I'm* not a squeamy squirrel.

KEITH. Anybody seen the girl since?

DOT. Yes.

HAROLD. Well?

DOT. She's just sitting there.

CHRISTINE. [*In a hard voice*] As we're all doing.

DOT. She's so soft, that's what's so horrible. If one could only feel——!

KEITH. She's got to face the music like the rest of us.

DOT. Music! Squeaks! Ugh! The whole thing's like a concertina, and some one jigging it!

> *They all turn as the door opens, and a* FOOTMAN *enters with a tray of whiskey, gin, lemons, and soda water. In dead silence the* FOOTMAN *puts the tray down.*

HAROLD. [*Forcing his voice*] Did you get a run, Ronny? [*As* KEITH *nods*] What point?

KEITH. Eight mile.

FOOTMAN. Will you take tea, sir?

KEITH. No, thanks, Charles!

> *In dead silence again the* FOOTMAN *goes out, and they all look after him.*

HAROLD. [*Below his breath*] Good Gad! That's a squeeze of it!

KEITH. What's our line of country to be?

CHRISTINE. All depends on father.

KEITH. Sir William's between the devil and the deep sea, as it strikes me.

CHRISTINE. He'll simply forbid it utterly, of course.

KEITH. H'm! Hard case! Man who reads family prayers, and lessons on Sunday forbids son to——

CHRISTINE. Ronny!

KEITH. Great Scott! I'm not saying Bill ought to marry her. She's got to stand the racket. But your Dad will have a tough job to take up that position.

DOT. Awfully funny!

CHRISTINE. What on earth d'you mean, Dot?

DOT. Morality in one eye, and your title in the other!

CHRISTINE. Rubbish!

HAROLD. You're all reckoning without your Bill.

KEITH. Ye-es. Sir William can cut him off; no mortal power can help the title going down, if Bill chooses to be such a——

> [*He draws in his breath with a sharp hiss.*

HAROLD. I won't take what Bill ought to have; nor would any of you girls, I should think——

CHRISTINE *and* DOT. Of course not!

KEITH. [*Patting his wife's arm*] Hardly the point, is it?

DOT. If it wasn't for mother! Freda's just as much of a lady as most girls. Why shouldn't he marry her, and go to Canada? It's what he's really fit for.

HAROLD. Steady on, Dot!

DOT. Well, imagine him in Parliament! That's what he'll come to, if he stays here—jolly for the country!

CHRISTINE. Don't be cynical! We must find a way of stopping Bill.

DOT. *Me* cynical!

CHRISTINE. Let's go and beg him, Ronny!

KEITH. No earthly! The only hope is in the girl.

DOT. She hasn't the stuff in her!

HAROLD. I say! What price young Dunning! Right about face! Poor old Dad!

CHRISTINE. It's past joking, Harold!

DOT. [*Gloomily*] Old Studdenham's better than most relations by marriage!

KEITH. Thanks!

CHRISTINE. It's ridiculous—monstrous! It's fantastic!

HAROLD. [*Holding up his hand*] There's his horse going round. He's in!

> *They turn from listening to the sound, to see* LADY
> CHESHIRE *coming from the billiard-room. She
> is very pale. They all rise and* DOT *puts an*

arm round her; while KEITH *pushes forward
his chair.* JOAN *and* LATTER *too have come
stealing back.*

LADY CHESHIRE. Thank you, Ronny!

[*She sits down.*

DOT. Mother, you're shivering! Shall I get you a
fur?

LADY CHESHIRE. No, thanks, dear!

DOT. [*In a low voice*] Play up, mother darling!

LADY CHESHIRE. [*Straightening herself*] What sort of
a run, Ronny?

KEITH. Quite fair, M'm. Brazier's to Caffyn's Dyke,
good straight line.

LADY CHESHIRE. And the young horse?

KEITH. Carries his ears in your mouth a bit, that's
all. [*Putting his hand on her shoulder*] Cheer up, Mem-
Sahib!

CHRISTINE. Mother, *must* anything be said to father?
Ronny thinks it all depends on *her*. Can't you use your
influence? [LADY CHESHIRE *shakes her head.*

CHRISTINE. But, mother, it's desperate.

DOT. Shut up, Chris! Of course mother can't. We
simply couldn't beg her to let us off!

CHRISTINE. There must be *some* way. What do you
think in your heart, mother?

DOT. Leave mother alone!

CHRISTINE. It must be faced, now or never.

DOT. [*In a low voice*] Haven't you any self-respect?

CHRISTINE. We shall be the laughing-stock of the
whole county. Oh! mother do speak to her! You

know it'll be misery for both of them. [LADY CHESHIRE *bows her head*] Well, then?

        [LADY CHESHIRE *shakes her head.*

CHRISTINE. Not even for Bill's sake?

DOT. Chris!

CHRISTINE. Well, for heaven's sake, speak to Bill again, mother! We ought all to go on our knees to him.

LADY CHESHIRE. He's with your father now.

HAROLD. Poor old Bill!

CHRISTINE. [*Passionately*] He didn't think of *us!* That wretched girl!

LADY CHESHIRE. Chris!

CHRISTINE. There are limits!

LADY CHESHIRE. Not to self-control.

CHRISTINE. No, mother! I can't—I never shall—Something must be done! You know what Bill is. He rushes at things so, when he gets his head down. Oh! do try! It's only fair to her, and all of us!

LADY CHESHIRE. [*Painfully*] There are things one can't do.

CHRISTINE. But it's Bill! I know you can make her give him up, if you'll only say all you can. And, after all, what's coming won't affect her as if she'd been a lady. Only *you* can do it, mother. Do back me up, all of you! It's the only way!

      Hypnotised by their private longing for what CHRISTINE *has been urging they have all fixed their eyes on* LADY CHESHIRE, *who looks from face to face, and moves her hands as if in physical pain.*

CHRISTINE. [*Softly*] Mother!

    LADY CHESHIRE *suddenly rises, looking towards the billiard-room door, listening. They all follow her eyes. She sits down again, passing her hand over her lips, as* SIR WILLIAM *enters. His hunting clothes are splashed; his face very grim and set. He walks to the fire without a glance at any one, and stands looking down into it. Very quietly, every one but* LADY CHESHIRE *steals away.*

LADY CHESHIRE. What have you done?

SIR WILLIAM. *You* there!

LADY CHESHIRE. Don't keep me in suspense!

SIR WILLIAM. The fool! My God! Dorothy! I didn't think I had a blackguard for a son, who was a fool into the bargain.

LADY CHESHIRE. [*Rising*] If he were a blackguard he would not be what you call a fool.

SIR WILLIAM. [*After staring angrily, makes her a slight bow*] Very well!

LADY CHESHIRE. [*In a low voice*] Bill, don't be harsh. It's all too terrible.

SIR WILLIAM. Sit down, my dear.

    [*She resumes her seat, and he turns back to the fire.*

SIR WILLIAM. In all my life I've never been face to face with a thing like this. [*Gripping the mantelpiece so hard that his hands and arms are seen shaking*] You ask me to be calm. I am trying to be. Be good enough in turn not to take his part against me.

LADY CHESHIRE. Bill!

SIR WILLIAM. I am trying to think. I understand that you've known this—piece of news since this morning. I've known it ten minutes. Give me a little time, please. [*Then, after a silence*] Where's the girl?

LADY CHESHIRE. In the workroom.

SIR WILLIAM. [*Raising his clenched fist*] What in God's name is he about?

LADY CHESHIRE. What have you said to him?

SIR WILLIAM. Nothing—by a miracle. [*He breaks away from the fire and walks up and down*] My family goes back to the thirteenth century. Nowadays they laugh at that! I don't! Nowadays they laugh at everything—they even laugh at the word lady—I married *you*, and I don't. . . . Married his mother's maid! By George! Dorothy! I don't know what we've done to deserve this; it's a death blow! I'm not prepared to sit down and wait for it. By Gad! I am not. [*With sudden fierceness*] There are plenty in these days who'll be glad enough for this to happen; plenty of these d——d Socialists and Radicals, who'll laugh their souls out over what they haven't the bowels to see's a—tragedy. I say it *would* be a tragedy; for you, and me, and all of us. You and I were brought up, and we've brought the children up, with certain beliefs, and wants, and habits. A man's past—his traditions—he can't get rid of them. They're—they're himself! [*Suddenly*] It shan't go on.

LADY CHESHIRE. What's to prevent it?

SIR WILLIAM. I utterly forbid this piece of madness. I'll stop it.

LADY CHESHIRE. But the thing we can't stop.

SIR WILLIAM. Provision must be made.

LADY CHESHIRE. The unwritten law!

SIR WILLIAM. What! [*Suddenly perceiving what she is alluding to*] You're thinking of young—young—— [*Shortly*] I don't see the connection.

LADY CHESHIRE. What's so awful, is that the boy's trying to do what's loyal—and we—his father and mother—!

SIR WILLIAM. I'm not going to see my eldest son ruin his life. I must think this out.

LADY CHESHIRE. [*Beneath her breath*] I've tried that —it doesn't help.

SIR WILLIAM. This girl, who was born on the estate, had the run of the house—brought up with money earned from me—nothing but kindness from all of us; she's broken the common rules of gratitude and decency—she lured him on, I haven't a doubt!

LADY CHESHIRE. [*To herself*] In a way, I suppose.

SIR WILLIAM. What! It's ruin. We've always been here. Who the deuce are we if we leave this place? D'you think we could stay? Go out and meet everybody just as if nothing had happened? Good-bye to any prestige, political, social, or anything! This is the sort of business nothing can get over. I've seen it before. As to that other matter—it's soon forgotten—constantly happening—Why, my own grandfather——!

LADY CHESHIRE. Does he help?

SIR WILLIAM. [*Stares before him in silence—suddenly*] You must go to the girl. She's soft. She'll never hold out against you.

LADY CHESHIRE. I did before I knew what was in front of her—I said all I could. I can't go again now. I can't do it, Bill.

SIR WILLIAM. What *are* you going to do, then—fold your hands? [*Then as* LADY CHESHIRE *makes a move- ment of distress.*] If he marries her, I've done with him. As far as I'm concerned he'll cease to exist. The title— I can't help. My God! Does that meet your wishes?

LADY CHESHIRE. [*With sudden fire*] You've no right to put such an alternative to me. I'd give ten years of my life to prevent this marriage. I'll go to Bill. I'll beg him on my knees.

SIR WILLIAM. Then why can't you go to the girl? She deserves no consideration. It's not a question of morality. Morality be d——d!

LADY CHESHIRE. But not self-respect.

SIR WILLIAM. What! You're his mother!

LADY CHESHIRE. I've tried; I [*putting her hand to her throat*] can't get it out.

SIR WILLIAM. [*Staring at her*] You won't go to her? It's the only chance. [LADY CHESHIRE *turns away.*

SIR WILLIAM. In the whole course of our married life, Dorothy, I've never known you set yourself up against me. I resent this, I warn you—I resent it. Send the girl to me. I'll do it myself.

> *With a look back at him* LADY CHESHIRE *goes out into the corridor.*

SIR WILLIAM. This is a nice end to my day!

> *He takes a small china cup from off the mantel- piece: it breaks with the pressure of his hand,*

and falls into the fireplace. While he stands looking at it blankly, there is a knock.

SIR WILLIAM. Come in!

FREDA enters from the corridor.

SIR WILLIAM. I've asked you to be good enough to come, in order that—[*pointing to chair*] You may sit down.

> *But though she advances two or three steps, she does not sit down.*

SIR WILLIAM. This is a sad business.

FREDA. [*Below her breath*] Yes, Sir William.

SIR WILLIAM. [*Becoming conscious of the depths of feeling before him*] I—er—are you attached to my son?

FREDA. [*In a whisper*] Yes.

SIR WILLIAM. It's very painful to me to have to do this. [*He turns away from her and speaks to the fire. I sent for you—to—ask—*[*quickly*] How old are you?

FREDA. Twenty-two.

SIR WILLIAM. [*More resolutely*] Do you expect me to —sanction such a mad idea as a marriage?

FREDA. I don't expect anything.

SIR WILLIAM. You know—you haven't earned the right to be considered.

FREDA. Not yet!

SIR WILLIAM. What! That oughtn't to help you! On the contrary. Now brace yourself up, and listen to me!

> *She stands waiting to hear her sentence. SIR WILLIAM looks at her; and his glance gradually wavers.*

SIR WILLIAM. I've not a word to say for my son. He's behaved like a scamp.

FREDA. Oh! no!

SIR WILLIAM. [*With a silencing gesture*] At the same time— What made you forget yourself? You've no excuse, you know.

FREDA. No.

SIR WILLIAM. You'll deserve all you'll get. Confound it! To expect me to— It's intolerable! Do you know where my son is?

FREDA. [*Faintly*] I think he's in the billiard-room with my lady.

SIR WILLIAM. [*With renewed resolution*] I wanted to —to put it to you—as a—as a—what! [*Seeing her stand so absolutely motionless, looking at him, he turns abruptly, and opens the billiard-room door*] I'll speak to him first. Come in here, please! [*To* FREDA] Go in, and wait!

LADY CHESHIRE *and* BILL *come in, and* FREDA *passing them, goes into the billiard-room to wait.*

SIR WILLIAM. [*Speaking with a pause between each sentence*] Your mother and I have spoken of this—calamity. I imagine that even you have some dim perception of the monstrous nature of it. I must tell you this: If you do this mad thing, you fend for yourself. You'll receive nothing from me now or hereafter. I consider that only due to the position our family has always held here. Your brother will take your place. We shall get on as best we can without you. [*There is a dead silence, till he adds sharply*] Well!

BILL. I shall marry her.

LADY CHESHIRE. Oh! Bill! Without love—without anything!

BILL. All right, mother! [*To* SIR WILLIAM] You've mistaken your man, sir. Because I'm a rotter in one way, I'm not necessarily a rotter in all. You put the butt end of the pistol to Dunning's head yesterday, you put the other end to mine to-day. Well! [*He turns round to go out*] Let the d—d thing off!

LADY CHESHIRE. Bill!

BILL. [*Turning to her*] I'm not going to leave her in the lurch.

SIR WILLIAM. Do me the justice to admit that I have not attempted to persuade you to.

BILL. No! you've chucked me out. I don't see what else you could have done under the circumstances. It's quite all right. But if you wanted me to throw her over, father, you went the wrong way to work, that's all; neither you nor I are very good at seeing consequences.

SIR WILLIAM. Do you realise your position?

BILL. [*Grimly*] I've a fair notion of it.

SIR WILLIAM. [*With a sudden outburst*] You have none—not the faintest, brought up as you've been.

BILL. I didn't bring myself up.

SIR WILLIAM. [*With a movement of uncontrolled anger, to which his son responds*] You—ungrateful young dog!

LADY CHESHIRE. How can you—both?

[*They drop their eyes, and stand silent.*

SIR WILLIAM. [*With grimly suppressed emotion*] I am speaking under the stress of very great pain—some consideration is due to me. This is a disaster which I never expected to have to face. It is a matter which I naturally can never hope to forget. I shall carry this down to my death. We shall all of us do that. I have had the misfortune all my life to believe in our position here —to believe that we counted for something—that the country wanted us. I have tried to do my duty by that position. I find in one moment that it is gone—smoke —gone. My philosophy is not equal to that. To countenance this marriage would be unnatural.

BILL. I know. I'm sorry. I've got her into this— I don't see any other way out. It's a bad business for me, father, as well as for you——

He stops, seeing that JACKSON *has come in, and is standing there waiting.*

JACKSON. Will you speak to Studdenham, Sir William? It's about young Dunning.

After a moment of dead silence, SIR WILLIAM *nods, and the butler withdraws.*

BILL. [*Stolidly*] He'd better be told.

SIR WILLIAM. He shall be.

STUDDENHAM *enters, and touches his forehead to them all with a comprehensive gesture.*

STUDDENHAM. Good evenin', my lady! Evenin', Sir William!

STUDDENHAM. Glad to be able to tell you, the young man's to do the proper thing. Asked me to let you know, Sir William. Banns'll be up next Sunday. [*Struck by the silence, he looks round at all three in turn, and suddenly seeing that* LADY CHESHIRE *is shivering*] Beg pardon, my lady, you're shakin' like a leaf!

BILL. [*Blurting it out*] I've a painful piece of news for you, Studdenham; I'm engaged to your daughter. We're to be married at once.

STUDDENHAM. I—don't—understand you—sir.

BILL. The fact is, I've behaved badly; but I mean to put it straight.

STUDDENHAM. I'm a little deaf. Did you say—my daughter?

SIR WILLIAM. There's no use mincing matters, Studdenham. It's a thunderbolt—young Dunning's case over again.

STUDDENHAM. I don't rightly follow. She's—You've—! I must see my daughter. Have the goodness to send for her, m'lady.

> LADY CHESHIRE *goes to the billiard-room, and calls:* "FREDA, *come here, please.*"

STUDDENHAM. [*To* SIR WILLIAM] You tell me that my daughter's in the position of that girl owing to your son? Men ha' been shot for less.

BILL. If you like to have a pot at me, Studdenham—you're welcome.

STUDDENHAM. [*Averting his eyes from* BILL *at the sheer idiocy of this sequel to his words*] I've been in your service five and twenty years, Sir William; but this is man to man—this is!

SIR WILLIAM. I don't deny that, Studdenham.

STUDDENHAM. [*With eyes shifting in sheer anger*] No—'twouldn't be very easy. Did I understand him to say that he offers her marriage?

SIR WILLIAM. You did.

STUDDENHAM. [*Into his beard*] Well—that's something! [*Moving his hands as if wringing the neck of a bird*] I'm tryin' to see the rights o' this.

SIR WILLIAM. [*Bitterly*] You've all your work cut out for you, Studdenham.

Again STUDDENHAM *makes the unconscious wringing movement with his hands.*

LADY CHESHIRE. [*Turning from it with a sort of horror*] Don't, Studdenham! Please!

STUDDENHAM. What's that, m'lady?

LADY CHESHIRE. [*Under her breath*] Your—your—hands.

While STUDDENHAM *is still staring at her,* FREDA *is seen standing in the doorway, like a black ghost.*

STUDDENHAM. Come here! You! [FREDA *moves a few steps towards her father*] When did you start this?

FREDA. [*Almost inaudibly*] In the summer, father.

LADY CHESHIRE. Don't be harsh to her!

STUDDENHAM. Harsh! [*His eyes again move from side to side as if pain and anger had bewildered them. Then looking sideways at* FREDA, *but in a gentler voice*] And when did you tell him about—what's come to you?

FREDA. Last night.

STUDDENHAM. Oh! [*With sudden menace*] You young——! [*He makes a convulsive movement of one hand; then, in the silence, seems to lose grip of his thoughts, and puts his hand up to his head*] I want to clear me mind a bit—I don't see it plain at all. [*Without looking at* BILL] 'Tis said there's been an offer of marriage?

BILL. I've made it, I stick to it.

STUDDENHAM. Oh! [*With slow, puzzled anger*] I want time to get the pith o' this. You don't say anything, Sir William?

SIR WILLIAM. The facts are all before you.

STUDDENHAM. [*Scarcely moving his lips*] M'lady?

[LADY CHESHIRE *is silent.*

STUDDENHAM. [*Stammering*] My girl was—was good enough for any man. It's not for him that's—that's—to look down on her. [*To* FREDA] You hear the handsome offer that's been made you? Well? [FREDA *moistens her lips and tries to speak, but cannot*] If nobody's to speak a word, we won't get much forrarder. I'd like for you to say what's in your mind, Sir William.

SIR WILLIAM. I—If my son marries her he'll have to make his own way.

STUDDENHAM. [*Savagely*] I'm not puttin' thought to that.

SIR WILLIAM. I didn't suppose you were, Studdenham. It appears to rest with your daughter. [*He suddenly takes out his handkerchief, and puts it to his forehead*] Infernal fires they make up here!

LADY CHESHIRE, *who is again shivering desperately, as if with intense cold, makes a violent attempt to control her shuddering.*

STUDDENHAM. [*Suddenly*] There's luxuries that's got to be paid for. [*To* FREDA] Speak up, now.

> FREDA *turns slowly and looks up at* SIR WILLIAM; *he involuntarily raises his hand to his mouth. Her eyes travel on to* LADY CHESHIRE, *who faces her, but so deadly pale that she looks as if she were going to faint. The girl's gaze passes on to* BILL, *standing rigid, with his jaw set.*

FREDA. I want—[*Then flinging her arm up over her eyes, she turns from him*] No!

SIR WILLIAM. Ah!

> *At that sound of profound relief,* STUDDENHAM, *whose eyes have been following his daughter's, moves towards* SIR WILLIAM, *all his emotion turned into sheer angry pride.*

STUDDENHAM. Don't be afraid, Sir William! We want none of you! She'll not force herself where she's not welcome. She may ha' slipped her good name, but she'll keep her proper pride. I'll have no *charity marriage* in my family.

SIR WILLIAM. Steady, Studdenham!

STUDDENHAM. If the young gentleman has tired of her in three months, as a blind man can see by the looks of him—she's not for him!

BILL. [*Stepping forward*] I'm ready to make it up to her.

STUDDENHAM. Keep back, there? [*He takes hold of* FREDA, *and looks around him*] Well! She's not the first this has happened to since the world began,

an' she won't be the last.   Come away, now, come
away!

>*Taking* FREDA *by the shoulders, he guides her
towards the door.*

SIR WILLIAM. D——n it, Studdenham!   Give us
credit for something!

STUDDENHAM. [*Turning—his face and eyes lighted up
by a sort of smiling snarl*] Ah! I do that, Sir William.
But there's things that can't be undone!

>[*He follows* FREDA *out.*
>*As the door closes,* SIR WILLIAM'S *calm gives way.
He staggers past his wife, and sinks heavily,
as though exhausted, into a chair by the fire.*
BILL, *following* FREDA *and* STUDDENHAM, *has
stopped at the shut door.* LADY CHESHIRE
*moves swiftly close to him.   The door of the
billiard-room is opened, and* DOT *appears.   With
a glance round, she crosses quickly to her mother.*

DOT. [*In a low voice*] Mabel's just going, mother'
[*Almost whispering*] Where's Freda?   Is it—— Has
she really had the pluck?

>LADY CHESHIRE *bending her head for* "*Yes,*"
*goes out into the billiard-room.   DOT clasps her
hands together, and standing there in the middle
of the room, looks from her brother to her father,
from her father to her brother.   A quaint little
pitying smile comes on her lips.   She gives a
faint shrug of her shoulders.*

The curtain falls.